ISRAELI ALBUM

Devotion to the Promised Land

ISRAELI

(TEXT BY) DOV BEN-ABBA
FOREWORD BY ISRAEL GALILI
MINISTER OF INFORMATION

Devotion to the Promised Land

ALBUM

HARRY N. ABRAMS, INC. *PUBLISHERS* NEW YORK

EDITOR: Amir Gilboa

ART EDITOR: N. Avnon

PHOTOS: Aldan, Ami, Avnon, Brukarz, Aviel, Bahir, Braun, Brauner, Carmi, Cohn, Csasznik, Fernbach, Frank, Friedman, Freundlich, Fuchs, Government Information Office, Gross, Haris, Hartmann, Herz, Levi, Lotan, May, Merom, Mirlin-Yaron, Pinn, Prior, Rothenberg, Rubinger, Sadeh, Sharon, Shweig, Schlesinger, Tal, Volk, Yadin. "Bamahane—Photo Studio"

Library of Congress Catalog Card Number: 68-20853

Copyright 1967 by Massada Ltd., Israel
Printed and bound in Israel by PELI-P.E.C. Printing Works Ltd.

FOREWORD

The following pages show the country which Israel's fighting men and women fought to save from total destruction in June 1967. This is the land whose population was spared the unspeakable horrors of mass murder. The pictures in this album show the land itself and the people who lovingly and devotedly gave it the image which it presents to the world today.

Various factors forged the character of the people who comprise this land and who placed their own individual stamp upon it: an ardent love of country, desolate as some of it still is; love of the Jewish people and the values which made it unique in world history; the impact of the Bible; home life and the schools; the inspiration of modern Hebrew literature; the conviction that it has the moral power to establish a better society; and the awareness of the necessity to build a home where the Jewish people can develop its own spiritual qualities undisturbed.

These are the forces which endowed Israel's soldiers and civilians with the qualities which triumphed over the evil bent on destroying them.

The photographs speak to the eye and the heart, for they radiate a love of the Land Israel.

ISRAEL GALILI
MINISTER OF INFORMATION

Jerusalem, Tammuz 5727—July 1967

ISRAELI ALBUM

Devotion to the Promised Land

ON A HOT DAY IN AUGUST in the year 70 of the Common Era, crackling flames leaped skyward and dark clouds of smoke drifted up over the blackened buildings of Jerusalem. Chained to one another, the survivors of the Roman siege, prodded by spears still red with blood, limped off on the first stage of their journey to Rome and the arenas where they would entertain the populace.

To commemorate his victory over the stubborn Jews, the Roman emperor Titus had an arch erected in Rome. One of the panels shows the Jewish captives and Roman soldiers carrying off the sacred vessels of the Temple they had destroyed. For the Jews, this was the beginning of a long, weary, seemingly endless march into a darkness which thickened and became more harrowing as the years wore on.

To proclaim his triumph to the world, Titus had coins struck showing a woman symbolizing Judea sitting with bowed head. Above her an inscription said *Iudaea capta,* "Judea has been taken."

For nineteen centuries the shame and horror of *Iudaea capta* weighed like a crushing burden on the bowed heads and shoulders of countless Jews across the sun-baked deserts of the Middle East and North Africa, the dreary gloom of ghettos in Italy, France, and Spain, the terror-ridden Jewish streets of medieval Germany, and the dismal, cold hopelessness of the Russian empire.

But everywhere the harsh night of exile was softened by the soothing fingers of a glow which never went out. On the steep, brown, dusty plateau of Masada near the Dead Sea, the Zealots who lifted up their swords to deliver a quick, merciful blow to kill their fellows, their wives, and children before the Romans arrived in the year 73 C.E. had a final vision of Zion restored.

In fifteenth-century Spain, mothers who clapped their hands over the mouths of their young infants to keep their cries from reaching the mobs outside caught a glimpse in some corner of their mind of peace and quiet under a shady vine arbor on a Judean hill. Was it a vivid memory handed down by past traditions or a clairvoyant peep into the distant future?

Rabbis in the Rhineland listened with pounding hearts to the clatter of Crusader armor and the subsequent roar of countless throats thirsting for blood and shrieking "Hep, Hep," the gruesome initials for *Hierosolyma est perdita*—Jerusalem is destroyed. For what better way was there to strike at the soul of the Jew than to jeer at the loss of what was most precious to him?

And when a little Jewish boy would come running home with blood streaming from his head and his ears ringing with the sounds of hate, his mother would quickly close the shutters against the cold Russian night and comfort him with tales of a warm land where once his people had lived like other peoples and would one day do so again. Behind a huge brick oven he would then sit with his father and steep himself in the lore and history of the people of Israel. In the large oblong pages of the Talmud, surrounded by commentaries in small type, he would immerse himself in laws of sowing and harvesting, of jurisprudence and business ethics, of relations with one's fellow man, all vividly redolent of life in the hills of Judea and Samaria, the mountains of Galilee, and the plain of Sharon.

For a Jew living in the agonizing aftermath of *Iudaea capta,* that Judea was as much a part of his everyday life as his heartbeat, as the name of Jerusalem which he breathed in his prayers three times daily, with a tremor in his breast and a cold longing in his stomach. Only the lips of the Jew whispered the words of such an oath as "If I forget thee, O Jerusalem, let my right hand forget her cunning. Let my tongue cleave to the roof of my mouth, if I remember thee not; if I set not Jerusalem above my chiefest joy."

And so it came about that men and women who sought an answer to the "why's" hurled at them in desperation by fathers and mothers, sons and daughters, found themselves transformed into sleepwalkers stalking through the mists of an electrifying vision. Their eyes were fixed on an emblem bearing words of redemption. They saw a silver medallion bearing the inscription "Israel liberated."

And one day, their sons and grandsons opened their eyes and saw that it was so. They heard the words of the Psalmist, of their ancient leader, whose voice had borne the clarion call of freedom down the ages and through all the lands of their wandering. In the language in which King David himself had spoken of love and life, of war and peace, of glory and of consolation for man's fate, their lips fluently said the words: "Our feet are standing within thy gates, O Jerusalem; Jerusalem, that art builded as a city that is compact together."

Both the synagogue preacher in Eastern Europe and the eager listeners bending forward to hear how warm it was in the Holy Land and how pure the air was there and how beautiful the countryside knew that they were indulging in wishful thinking to find solace from the harshness of everyday living. They knew that the land of Israel was a rock-covered, sparsely populated country denuded of trees and inhabited by people living a primitive existence and ridden by disease, ignorance, and stagnation. But the dream of what it had been and the enchantment of what it would be infused reality with a golden glow, and wherever they happened to be, they continued to celebrate holidays and rituals expressly applicable to their ancient, remote homeland.

And if the resurrection described in Orthodox tradition were truly to take place in Jerusalem —just as the resurrection of the people in its resurrected land had come true—this is what the myriads come to life again would see.

From Mount Scopus and the Mount of Olives they would look down on the pattern of white and rose buildings stretching westward to the horizon and embracing a Jerusalem of a quarter of a million people. King Solomon would not recognize the mosques on the area where his Temple had stood, nor would the walls and the prominence of Mount Zion appear familiar. But this is still the capital of Israel. Here, in the Knesset, the 120 elected representatives of the nation meet to make laws. In the stately assembly hall, men and women from every walk of life—farmers, merchants, lawyers, industrialists, rabbis, and teachers—decide the nature of the country's existence. Their faces molded in racial strains reflecting the wide range of the Jews' wandering, they argue, cajole, and orate in the language of King David and the prophet Isaiah, enunciated in a dozen different accents.

The legislators of Israel are elected every four years. Everyone who has reached the age of eighteen—the age when each young man and woman takes up arms in his country's defense— may vote. Sometimes the debates are bitter, and, hearing the shouting, one can hardly believe that less than a century ago the Hebrew language in which they so vividly express every aspect of life and living was congealed in books and reserved for prayer. The discussions are heated because numerous views are expressed on every possible topic. Israel is a democracy, and each person can choose to support a party voicing his opinions, from the extreme left to the far right, from left-wing Socialist to ultra-Orthodox, and all the shadings in between.

The government—the cabinet—consists of a coalition of several parties. Its head is the prime minister. Israel also has a president, who is elected by the Knesset for a five-year term to serve as the titular head of state.

The various departments of the government—the ministries—are located in Jerusalem, except for the Defense Ministry, which is in Tel Aviv. An industrialist who wishes to expand his plant manufacturing transistor radios is glad to leave the muggy heat of Tel Aviv on the coast for a ride into the winy mountain air of Jerusalem to meet with an official of the Ministry of Commerce and Industry. A school principal who is not satisfied with a geography book which the Ministry of Education and Culture requires him to use comes to Jerusalem to air his complaints.

But not only persons with business come to Jerusalem. Thousands of Israelis flock to the capital to visit its museums, walk in the narrow, winding, noisy streets of the old walled city, admire the modern structures of concrete, stone, and glass of the Hebrew University, and marvel at the Hadassah hospital on a hill just outside the city. In the bustling streets, echoing with heavy motor traffic and bustling crowds, Talmudic students in long black coats, with black bowlers wedged over long earlocks, lower their eyes at the approach of a girl vigorously swinging her bare legs under a miniskirt. In Israel, the old and the new are constantly meeting. There is a variety in ideas, architecture, clothing styles, and foods found in few places in the world.

And the diversity extends to the climate as well. Sitting on a balcony and looking at the bluish hills of Moab to the east on a September afternoon, a Jerusalemite feels a chill. His thermometer tells him it is 70 degrees Fahrenheit. He gets into his car and drives down along a winding road thrusting through walls of sandstone and grayish earth until, less than half an hour later, he takes a dip in the Dead Sea. Half-submerged in the water, which is heavy with the concentration of numerous minerals—potash, bromides, and other compounds—he is reluctant to emerge into the air with its 90-degree heat. Perhaps tomorrow it will be cooler. He turns on his radio, twisting the dial to see what one of Israel's three broadcasting bands has to offer. Maybe one of them will be announcing the temperatures. The army radio is playing swing music. The Voice of Israel's A Network has a lecture on spraying cotton fields. But its B Network has just what he wants.

The throaty voice of a girl is reading off the temperatures in various parts of the country. Our Jerusalemite is impatient, for the announcer begins in the north and works her way down, coming to Jerusalem and the Judean Hills somewhere near the end. As he listens, he suddenly becomes aware of the extent of climatic variation in his country. The mellow voice reads: "On the Golan Plateau . . . Tiberias . . . Galilee . . . Haifa . . . the Coastal Plain . . . the Judean Foothills . . . the Samarian Hills . . . Gaza and Northern Sinai . . . Solomon's Bay . . ." He thinks, Solomon's Bay, *that* used to be called Sharm esh-Sheikh when our enemies tried to strangle our southern port at Eilat.

His thoughts drift to Eilat. At the upper end of the Red Sea's right arm, the city, geometrically laid out in quarters, with its wide streets, hotels, and seaside promenade, has been likened to a jewel. Its port is Israel's gateway to East and South Africa, India, and the Far East. To it crude petroleum is brought, which is then transferred by pipeline to Haifa, where it is refined for all the numerous uses of a twentieth-century economy. Israel's industries, motor transport, and commercial activities consume tremendous quantities of the black gold. But Israel, too, has oil wells, and in the process of drilling for oil in the tawny hills near the Dead Sea and in the gritty soil of the south, Israeli workmen have discovered large quantities of natural gas, which the potash works at the southern tip of the Dead Sea and the phosphate plants in the northern Negev find extremely useful as a fuel.

Everything in Israel seems to be in motion. Its men, women, and children all appear to be headed somewhere. Even sauntering crowds on a Saturday afternoon—the Sabbath—flow in a definite direction. Let us look down on Tel Aviv from the top of the thirty-two-story Migdal Shalom building any weekday morning. People in Israel are early risers. Partly it is the climate which is responsible for the custom of beginning work early and taking a two- or three-hour break in the early afternoon.

At 7 A.M. long lines of people are waiting beside the bus stops. Once in a while an angry shout is heard when someone furtively attempts to enter a bus ahead of the line. Many people share rides to work in taxis, which ply regular routes. And the traffic jams in which sweating drivers curse other sweating drivers rival the worst congestion of London, Paris, or New York.

In Haifa, in Tel Aviv, and less so in Jerusalem, men and women stream to factories to produce the goods which Israel needs for itself, and which the country exports abroad. Jews whose grandfathers peddled dry goods now operate machines producing airplane parts, assembling automobiles and television sets, and mixing plastic paints. Stripped to the waist, their faces grimy with sweat and dust, men with huge tongs pull incandescent steel bars out of a clattering machine. In another plant the stench of hot rubber hits the nostrils like a desert wind as the workmen stack rows and rows of tires along a wall. Spindles whirr to produce miles of cotton yarn. Women with sensitive fingers carefully tighten tiny screws to hold precision instruments together. Dwarfed by the large pipes they are inspecting, men meticulously search the concrete surfaces for defects to make sure they will not leak when laid in the ground to carry water from the north to the parched Negev.

Nearly 40 per cent of the working population of Israel is employed in industrial undertakings. The old accusation hurled at Jews, that they worked at jobs which were not basically necessary for the economic life of a country, is meaningless in Israel. Huge cement factories spouting gray smoke not only supply building materials for dwellings, office buildings, wharves, sidewalks, and bridges, but also bring in foreign exchange from the countries to which they are exported. An Israeli who studied engineering at the Haifa Technical Institute leaves his laboratory, where he works at improving the quality of special kinds of paper products, drives off in a car assembled in Israel and in which items such as the battery are locally manufactured, parks the vehicle in a garage of asbestos slabs produced in the country, rides up to his apartment in an elevator which Israeli workers constructed from locally produced parts, knocks on the smooth formica panel of a door all of which was fabricated in Israel, kisses the Israeli lipstick on the lips of his wife, who surprises him with a new dress and shoes designed and manufactured in Israel, and sits down before an Israeli-produced television set to eat a sumptuous dinner of foods grown and processed in Israel. If he overeats, the medicines he has to take later are also produced in a number of the country's outstanding pharmaceutical plants.

The total amount of goods and services Israel produces amounted to over three and one-half billion dollars in 1967. An important source of income for Israel is its export trade. Industrial exports bring in the largest part of this income. In many countries of the Western world, women wear diamonds which were polished in Israel. Foodstuffs, metal products, chemicals, clothing and textiles, minerals, and leather goods are shipped to many countries. Israeli refrigerators and air conditioners make life easier and more pleasant for numerous people throughout the world.

To handle its foreign trade, Israel has five ports—Haifa, Tel Aviv, Jaffa, Eilat, and Ashdod. Tel Aviv and Jaffa have been largely supplanted by the up-to-date facilities in the coastal city of Ashdod, in which the princes of the Philistines once ruled. The majority of goods shipped to and from Israel go through Haifa. This is where Israel's large merchant fleet of about seventy-five vessels is based and where visitors to the country arrive. Haifa, the country's third-largest city, has a population of nearly 210,000.

Haifa was the dream city of the founder of political Zionism, Theodor Herzl. There is a famous photograph of this handsome, black-bearded father of modern Israel, standing on a balcony and gazing off into the distance at an enchanting vision visible only to his penetrating eyes. Close friends of his say that he was seeing Haifa, not a small, dusty fishing village as it was then, but the gleaming, turbulent metropolis mantling Mount Carmel today.

Arrivals to Israel on the deck of a vessel slowing its engines before slipping into the port are charmed by the view of Haifa stretching from the port, with its cranes, installations, warehouses, and granaries, up to central Carmel, with its patterned streets and white buildings, and, still higher, to the wooded top checkered with homes and apartment houses. To the left, the huge cylindrical structures of the refineries underline the industrial nature of the city, ringed by Israel's principal factories.

An air of accomplishment, of people and machines doing something, pulsates in the salty air of the city. The roads north, east, and south look like vibrating conveyor belts from a distance, alive with moving vehicles.

Early in the morning, the highways leading to Haifa hum with the roar of motors and the rumble of heavy trucks as a stream of agricultural produce flows into the central markets for redistribution. Here and there, huge tankers full of milk draw to a halt in front of a red traffic light, and a mellow gurgle tells the bystander they are full. Nearly one billion eggs a year are produced, of which about a tenth are exported.

For a nation which until half a century ago was widely regarded as having neither an aptitude nor a desire to dig in the soil and make things grow, the Jews have accomplished a near miracle. The wide variety of foods produced by Israeli farmers are also a geographical index of the great diversity in climatic conditions. Just as in the United States, one can have both bananas and apples for desert. One can sink one's teeth into a colorful salad of native pears, avocados, watermelons, pomegranates, plums, and dates, and wash it down with grapefruit juice.

Most of the agricultural produce which Israelis now enjoy and which people in many European countries are proud to serve on their tables were entirely unknown in the country until several years ago. In Britain, the Scandinavian countries, and most of northwestern Europe, mention of the name Israel immediately elicits the thought of oranges. Israel's oranges have conquered Europe in an ever-growing flood. Israelis of all sizes, shapes, and colors begin climbing ladders set up against citrus trees in the fall and carefully pluck off more than 850,000 tons of fruit, of which 570,000 tons are sent abroad.

People who farm in Israel consider it a mission as well as good business. Somewhere back in every Israeli's mind there are dank, gloomy regions thick with folk memories of narrow ghettos where seeing the sky was an occasion for offering up a special prayer of thanks to God. The Israeli who tumbles out of a warm bed before sunrise to plow, or sow, or reap, or spread insecticides in the fields may grumble, but when the sun rises up beyond the mountains across the Jordan and sheds a glow over the fields and trees, and he fills his lungs with the cool air under the vast expanse of sky, he knows he is a free man. In every cell of his blood he knows that what the poet Hayyim Nahman Bialik said about a man having as much free sky over his head as he has soil under his feet is indisputably so.

The Israeli farmer knows many things, for his own development, his urge to be well-informed, and his cultural pleasures are as much a part of his existence as the plot of land over which he walks barefoot in order to feel closer to the soil. Some of the country's most respected intellectual leaders live in farm communities. This is especially so in the collective villages, of which there are 230. The Hebrew word *kibbutz*—"collective settlement"—has been incorporated in most of the world's major languages.

The *kibbutz* is based on the principle of economic and social equality for all. This means that the man emptying the garbage and the woman serving in the capacity similar to that of a mayor may live in the same kind of quarters, eat the same food in the communal dining room, attend the same lectures, movies, plays, and concerts, send their children to the same schools, have the same paid vacations, and wear clothes of whatever style and quality the *kibbutz* offers all its members. Parents of the members are supported by the settlement in quarters of their own. In some *kibbutzim* (the plural of *kibbutz*) the young children sleep in their parents' rooms or apartments; in others, they sleep in special children's homes under expert care.

All the members of a *kibbutz* have a voice in its government, women having equal rights with men, except that during prenatal and postnatal periods they are accorded special privileges regarding working hours, diet, and vacation. All the land, buildings, tools, equipment, furniture, and vehicles of a *kibbutz* belong to the entire membership. Everyone physically capable of working is assigned a job. All jobs rotate. A prominent writer may be assigned a year for writing a book and then may spend six months waiting on tables or tending the sheep. Members of the Knesset coming home on vacation often work in the large communal kitchen. No honest work is considered degrading, and this is the spirit in which the new generation is brought up.

Many *kibbutzim* are now well off. They have long since advanced beyond the harrowing difficulties of their early years, when they were beset by marauders, distressed by crop failures, and lived under the constant threat of shortages of food, water, clothing, and housing. Their large dining rooms, with modern fixtures, paintings, and furnishings, resemble country clubs. Halls for entertainment and celebrations bring to mind the spacious premises of prominent resorts. Many *kibbutzim* also conduct industries in order to augment their income. Some manufacture modern teak furniture, screws, electric motors, plastic dishes; some operate metal-working plants and repair shops for vehicles.

Collective living is not for everyone. Some people cannot stand eating in a dining room with large numbers of other people. There are mothers who feel their children will not eat unless they are with them, who want their offspring near them more hours than a *kibbutz* would allow. Others do not want to be dependent on a general meeting of all their neighbors to decide how much of an allowance children should have to spend in town, or what kind of mattress they should sleep on.

For such persons who still believe that a joint effort accomplishes more than the haphazard strivings of an individual, there is another type of farm village—the *moshav* or *moshav ovedim*. These so-called smallholders' settlements or co-operative villages are the predominant type of agricultural village in Israel. There are 370 of them. The flood of immigrants which swept into the country after the establishment of the State of Israel in May 1948 preferred this type of communal living to the *kibbutz*.

If you live in a *moshav* you own your home and a plot of land which you or your wife can cultivate. You may grow flowers, or you may devote it to producing radishes. However, certain plots are worked by all the members and the produce is sold by the group as a whole. Equipment such as tractors, motor vehicles, and farm machinery belongs to the entire village. In some *moshavim,* livestock and manufacturing enterprises are also the property of the group as a whole.

For the individual who wants more co-operation than the *moshav* has to offer and less collectivization than the *kibbutz,* there is the *moshav shittoofi,* or collective *moshav*. Here, too, the settler owns his own home, but the farming and the economic set-up, including the purchase and sale of whatever is needed, are directed by the group as a whole.

In all the co-operative villages, the land belongs not to the individual or the group, but to the Jewish National Fund. This fund, supported by contributions from abroad and by Israelis, purchases and develops land as the perpetual property of the Jewish people. The Fund leases this land for settlement. By 1965 it had prepared 75,000 acres for settlement and carried out reclamation projects to improve another 100,000 acres. Tens of thousands of people have been employed by the Jewish National Fund in redeeming the soil of the land of Israel. Under a scorching sun, their feet blistered by thorns and rocks, bitten by insects in malarial swamps, these unknown workers transformed the face of Israel.

The contrast between Galilee and the central region of the Samarian hills strikes one immediately, whether one drives through in a car or flies over in a plane. The area in which the Jewish National Fund planted over 75,000,000 trees is lush with the vigorous green freshness of swaying treetops; the rest—stony expanses of scrub, raddled earth, and monotonous sterility—injects a feeling of heaviness into the heart.

On the Sabbath, Saturday, the general day of rest, and on holidays—the Jewish holy days and festivals—the highways are crowded with cars of all makes and vintages heading for the seashore, wooded picnic areas, or national parks. Israelis have become a nation of avid picnickers. Road-building is hard put to keep up with the precipitous growth of motor vehicles. The government is always in the midst of an extensive series of projects for constructing modern highways linking the various parts of the country, and more and more four-lane roads tie Israel's far-flung regions into a single, cohesive region. In a single day, the motorist can sweep around wooded mountain roads, yield to the temptation to push his accelerator down to the floor on a straight road cutting across a lengthy strip of yellowish, gritty desert, and skirt inland bodies of water like the Sea of Galilee or the Dead Sea.

For the devout, Sabbaths and holidays are moving spiritual experiences. Where the Orthodox live, roads are closed for the day of rest, for the laws of the Bible and Talmud concerning absolute abstention from work of any kind are here strictly observed. In religious villages and in the cities where the Orthodox live, a mellow hush settles at sundown of the day preceding the day of rest, for, according to a time-honored Jewish tradition, a 24-hour day extends from sundown to sundown. The synagogues fill with worshipers dressed in their Sabbath best and aglow with the "extra soul" which a person is supposed to acquire on the Seventh Day, when God rested from creating the world.

The Sabbath tradition of a day of spiritual replenishment permeates the life of the entire country. Government offices, factories, stores, and bus and rail traffic close down. The radio gears its programs to the mood of a well-deserved rest for people who for five and a half days have been occupied with making a living. Readings from Biblical portions appropriate to each particular Sabbath are broadcast. There is cantoral music. Lectures on scientific and cultural subjects are delivered by authorities. An expert on current affairs analyzes local and international events. And there are always interviews with leading personalities and with a cross-section of the Israeli population. The Israel radio has proved itself an effective instrument for welding people from seventy countries into a single nation with common goals and a common identification. By presenting the people and letting each speak of his immediate problems in his own halting Hebrew, the radio throws into relief the difficulties shared by all newcomers to Israel, and demonstrates how each group overcomes them.

The torchlight in the glow of which all Israelis bask is the goal of *Kibbutz Galuyot*—the Ingathering of the Exiled Communities. The Law of Return passed by the Israeli Knesset confers the right to immigrate to Israel on every Jew. It is chiefly through immigration that the Jewish population of Israel now consists of nearly 2,400,000 persons. From some countries, such as Iraq and Yemen, nearly the entire Jewish population has been evacuated to Israel. For large numbers of these immigrants, the trip across space was also a journey through time. The 50,000 Yemenite Jews flown to Israel in 1949–50 not only traversed a long distance but also passed from the Middle Ages to the twentieth century. People who had never sat on a chair, slept in a bed, or seen a bathroom suddenly discovered themselves flying like birds, listening to voices speaking from another city, seeing at night by bright lights from glass containers, and cooking on gas stoves.

Although the stream of immigration has dwindled, Israel has new housing waiting for immigrants. Each newcomer is given initial aid in the form of simple furniture, food, and clothing. Every possible effort is made to find proper work for the immigrant. A special department of the government helps place professionals such as doctors, teachers, and engineers. For persons who must learn Hebrew quickly in order to begin working, there are special intensive courses with living-in facilities. Here you can meet dark-skinned Indians, blond Poles, and brown Iraqis—all Jews—sitting for five hours a day to acquire fluency in a language some of them would not have been able to recognize a year before. In their rooms, the students have no choice but to converse in Hebrew, at first haltingly, because they have no other means of communication. So friendships between Russian-speaking Jews and English-speaking Jews are formed; and in many cases, closer ties have been established between members of opposite sexes, which culminate in marriage. Such an "intermarriage" is another step in the direction of fusing the diverse immigrants into a single Israeli type.

One of the first facilities made available to each new immigrant is membership in a sickness fund. This means that he receives complete medical care for himself and his family. Should he or any member of his family require an X-ray, an operation, or advanced treatment of any kind, the sickness fund will take care of him free of charge. After being in the country three months, the immigrant affiliates with a sickness fund to which he pays a monthly sum, the amount depending on his income, for complete health insurance. Such health insurance is made available by the General Federation of Labor, the Histadrut, as well as by other labor groups and private societies. In addition to government and private hospitals with the most advanced facilities for treatment, Israel also has hospitals run by the sickness fund of the Histadrut, by the Hadassah organization, and by other organizations.

Jointly with the Hebrew University in Jerusalem, the Hadassah organization conducts a medical and dental school. With the slackening in immigration, the number of professional men coming to Israel has diminished, but the country has now reached the stage where it can provide every type of professional and technological education. The education system begins with the nursery school and is crowned by a number of universities. Elementary school attendance is compulsory for all. However, most teenagers continue on in secondary schools preparing them for the university, in vocational schools, and in agricultural schools. Although secondary school education is not free, there are numerous scholarships provided by both the government and other public bodies, which are available to students from large families, underprivileged communities from Africa and Asia, and youngsters with exceptional abilities.

Study of the Bible is a central feature of Israel's educational system. In nursery school, where the young child can scarcely pronounce some of the names, he becomes familiar with the leading personalities of the Old Testament. In the first grade, he studies a simplified version of the Pentateuch, and throughout his school career the Israeli youngster becomes imbued with the history, ethics, and spirit of the Bible. When a child in a Jerusalem school glances up from his book and lets his eyes run over the vale of Rephaim, where King David defeated the Philistines, the entire early period of Jewish history assumes for him the vividness of an event in which he is personally involved.

Israel's schools, which are conducted by the government, have a crowded curriculum. The pupils must not only learn the basic skills of everyday living, but must also be taught to feel themselves the bearers of a rich, ancient culture which has left an indelible stamp on Western civilization and determined the course of much of human history. Sitting in his classroom, the Israeli boy or girl learns how to be a happy, useful citizen; he learns to appreciate the natural beauties of his country; and he learns to understand basic scientific processes. But in addition, he must also study world history, geography, and philosophy, for he is a member of a people scattered over the length and breadth of the planet.

In addition to the regular government schools, there are parallel institutions where religious values are emphasized and the pupils are required to carry out Orthodox observances. They, too, study the Bible, but strictly as a revelation of Divine will. Prayers and synagogue play an important part in the curriculum.

After completing a course of secondary education, higher education may be pursued at the Hebrew University in Jerusalem, at Tel Aviv University, at Bar-Ilan University in Ramat Gan, or at the Haifa Technological Institute. In addition, there are smaller universities at Haifa and Beersheba. Should a young Israeli be so inclined, he can study anything from Chinese to nuclear physics. And should he be particularly endowed, he may engage in research at the Weizmann Institute of Science at Rehovot in such fields as isotopes, biological ultrastructure, or advanced electronics.

Israelis no longer stop to gape at black-skinned Africans conversing in fluent Hebrew, or at a Burmese talking to a South American in the language of King Solomon. Israel maintains a special educational program for foreign students, in addition to sending experts to teach in developing countries. In 1965, an average year, 2,153 students from 80 countries came to Israel to study everything from medicine to co-operative marketing. Of this number, 1,200 came from Africa, 398 from Latin America, 220 from Asia, and 335 from countries of the Mediterranean basin. Since the foreign students speak so many different languages, often their only means of communication with each other is through the medium of Hebrew.

Of the almost 320,000 non-Jews who are Israeli citizens, a large percentage are Christians of every existing denomination. The clang of church bells on Sundays and on Christian holy days sends a thrill of recognition through all Christian visitors to the Holy Land. On Christmas and Easter, pilgrims from the entire Western world throng Jerusalem, Bethlehem, and Nazareth to experience at first hand the presence of the shrines associated with the birth and Passion of Jesus of Nazareth. Many of the Christian denominations maintain their own schools. Government schools for Arabs are conducted in the Arabic language.

An ancient sect which at one time numbered many thousands but now consists of 400 persons—160 in Holon and 240 in the Biblical Shechem— still performs the time-honored rituals prescribed in the Old Testament to the letter. Thus, on Passover, they sacrifice the paschal lamb on Mount Gerizim, their holiest shrine.

But Israelis do not spend all their time working or studying—there are numerous extension courses for adults where a person can learn anything from bee-keeping to the problems of modern Japan. Israelis are also avid movie-goers. The cities and towns all have their motion picture theaters, where news and a feature film are shown three times a day. Most films are American, but many British, French, and Italian films are attended by large numbers of people. The films all have a Hebrew and French or English translation on the same screen. Israel's young movie industry is constantly expanding, and locally produced films in Hebrew draw large audiences.

The legitimate theater also has its adherents. In addition to 5 large, permanent companies, many cities have their own small groups presenting Israeli and foreign plays in translation and an occasional experimental piece. Plays are also presented in English, Yiddish, and other languages. Performances are generally played to a full house. The Israeli opera has many local artists as well as guest artists from abroad.

Long ago, the Arabs conferred on the Jews the title People of the Book—*Ahl el-Kitab*—and so they have remained to this day. Israel occupies first place in the world in the number of books sold annually per capita. Visitors to the country marvel at the number of book stores. More than one hundred publishers provide the Israeli population with about 1,500 new titles every year. Of these, at least one-fourth are translations of the best—and sometimes the worst—in world literature. Shortly after a best-seller casts its shadow across its own country, a Hebrew translation appears in Israel, to be grabbed from the book stores almost immediately.

Israelis have a strong sense of being part of the entire world and are intensely interested in what is going on in other countries, especially concerning Jews, relations with Israel, and attitudes toward the Arab-Israeli conflict. Fifteen daily newspapers in Hebrew and at least ten in other languages ranging from English to Hungarian and Arabic not only keep the population informed but also attempt to guide people's political thinking. One of the conspicuous signs of Israeli democracy is the absolute freedom of the press—except where security matters are concerned. Most political parties and factions have their own newspapers and periodicals presenting their particular point of view.

The press also publishes numerous informative articles on the various sciences. In addition, there are many periodicals for the professional, dealing with specific fields such as history, education, the exact sciences, public affairs, literature, and various trades and professions. Visitors from other countries find it hard to believe that Israel's thriving cultural life was almost non-existent half a century ago.

Although television was late in coming to the country, Israel has had educational television since March 1966. In many schools throughout the country, pupils impatiently wait for their lessons in arithmetic, English, or biology to be explained to them by a teacher in the little oblong box. From the number of television antennas on the roofs, one would not believe that Israel was one of the last countries to introduce its own television—and this, only in the aftermath of the Six-Day War of June 1967, to counteract the virulent anti-Israel propaganda of the neighboring countries. Even Israelis who knew no Arabic faithfully viewed programs from Cairo, Damascus, and Beirut; some sets even pick up Cyprus quite well.

The subscriptions to the concerts of the Israeli Philharmonic Orchestra are always sold out. This orchestra has the highest proportionate attendance of any in the world. Special recitals never have any difficulty selling tickets, and foreign entertainers are amazed at the response their presentations elicit. Israel has museums of world-wide renown in Jerusalem, Tel Aviv, and Haifa. In a number of towns and villages there are museums devoted to the locality—its geology, history, plant and animal life, and people. Everyone in Israel is an amateur archaeologist. Each relic and artifact of the past is ardently sought after, as if a people long separated from its native land needed as much physical evidence as it could unearth to strengthen its ties with the land of its fathers. Israel's museums are replete with vessels, implements, articles of clothing, and architectural specimens, testifying to the abiding attachment of the Israeli for his country's past.

To assure the country's survival, Israel has had to devote an inordinate proportion of its budget and manpower to defense. The constant threats of the Arab countries to annihilate Israel have made perpetual vigilance a prime condition for survival. Israel's secondary schools give the pupils a rigorous course of premilitary training. At the age of eighteen, all of the young men and women in the country—except those who for religious reasons do not serve—enter the armed forces. Men serve for two and one-half years, women for two.

The training is tough. Israel's most powerful weapon is the spirit of its manpower. In three wars for survival, the Israeli armed forces have shown that neither superior numbers nor quality of weapons and equipment decide the outcome. Victory in every case was determined by the devotion, fighting spirit, and skill of the troops. And Israeli officers lead their men into battle with the cry "Follow me!" instead of ordering them to advance.

Israel's army is a people's army. The entire nation is one in mind and body with its soldiers. After a conscript has completed his service, he returns for retraining periods every year until the age of 49. The bulk of the armed forces consists of reservists who can be called to the colors and equipped for grappling with the enemy in a matter of hours.

Resourcefulness and eagerness to attempt the unconventional characterize every branch of the service—infantry, artillery, paratroops, navy, and air force. And above all, the men are keenly aware that the future of an ancient people which has given much to the world and which has suffered much depends on them. When it comes to bracing themselves to repulse the onslaught of a foe proclaiming his intention of massacring the entire population, the people of Israel know they can depend only on themselves.

The Israeli armed forces also serve as a vital educational force in welding people from all parts of the globe into a single national entity. Newcomers are taught Hebrew and learn to identify themselves with their people, from which some of them have become alienated in a foreign environment. The army also sends teachers to the towns and villages of new immigrants to teach the older generation as well as youngsters Hebrew and the fundamentals of good citizenship and living in a modern, democratic society.

Israel wants to be allowed to grow, develop the resources of its land and people, and maintain the continuity of Jewry and Jewish culture. The People of Israel in the Land of Israel have in the past made enduring contributions to human civilization, and in the brief period of the modern state's existence have already demonstrated their ability to become active partners in the advancement of mankind.

ABOUT THE AUTHOR

DOV BEN-ABBA, M.Sc., is a native of Boston, Massachusetts. He was educated at Harvard University, the University of Pennsylvania, the Boston Hebrew Teachers College, and the Hebrew University at Jerusalem. A linguist, he has mastered a number of Semitic languages, including various dialects of spoken Arabic. He has long been a student of the Middle East, about which he has published articles and monographs in English, Hebrew, and Yiddish.

During World War II, Mr. Ben-Abba served with the United States Army Air Force and spent two years in Cairo. He has been living in Israel since 1947, and since 1950 has been associated with the United Press as correspondent in Israel, covering all major events in the country, including the Six-Day War of June 1967. Since 1952 he has been employed by the Massada Publishing Company in the capacity of writer, editor, and translator. Mr. Ben-Abba has directed the firm's research department since March 1966. In addition to editing a number of works published by the company, he served as Assistant Editor of the Standard Jewish Encyclopaedia and is a regular contributor to the Encyclopaedia Hebraica.

NOTE ON THE
BIBLICAL QUOTATIONS

To the people of modern Israel, the Holy Scriptures are both an ethical guide and an historical account of their land and tradition. Former Prime Minister David Ben-Gurion, remembering references to the copper mines of Solomon in the Old Testament, urged geologists to explore the possibilities in the regions so described —and copper deposits were subsequently discovered. Israel continues to look to the Bible for similar guidelines as it struggles to irrigate the arid fields—as King Hezekiah once did—and unearth new minerals from the "tops of ancient mountains."

It is therefore appropriate that the Old Testament serve as a source for the quotations that accompany these photographs of modern Israel. From this device we may observe some of the same relationships between daily life and spiritual inspiration that moved the ancient scribes. We will see the terrain, the wastes, and the cities as they saw them, and may appreciate the similes and metaphors they used as we realize how little has changed in the basic and undying nature of the ancient land.

All quotations are derived from the Holy Scriptures according to the Masoretic text, as published by the Menorah Press, Chicago.

At Basel I founded the Jewish State. If I were to say this openly today, I would meet with universal laughter. But within five years, perhaps, and certainly within fifty, everyone will see it.

THEODOR HERZL *1897*

Our feet are standing
Within thy gates, O Jerusalem;
Jerusalem, that art builded
As a city that is compact together...
Pray for the peace of Jerusalem...

PSALM 122:2-3, 6

The Wailing Wall after the liberation of Jerusalem

Thou didst turn for me my mourning into dancing...
O Lord my God, I will give thanks unto Thee for ever.

PSALM 30:12-13

...they that wait for the Lord shall renew their strength;
They shall mount up with wings as eagles...

ISAIAH 40:31

...We are journeying unto the place of which the LORD said: I will give it to you...

NUMBERS 10:29

And ye girded on every man his weapons of war...

DEUTERONOMY 1:41

And ye shall chase your enemies,
and they shall fall before you…

LEVITICUS 26:7

He maketh thy borders peace...

PSALM 147:14

The Golan Plateau

Thou hast remembered the earth, and watered her, greatly enriching her...   PSALM 65:10

Waterfall near Metullah

At midnight in the Artists' Club

*...the singers also [played] on
instruments of music, and led
the singing of praise.*

II CHRONICLES 23:13

*Sing unto Him a
new song;
Play skilfully amid
shouts of joy.*

PSALM 33:3

Concert in the Caesarea Amphitheater

Kibbutz kitchen in the southern Negev

...eat so much as is sufficient for thee...

PROVERB 25:16

The meadows are clothed with flocks...

PSALM 65:14

On the hills of Galilee

...a land whose stones are iron,
and out of whose hills
thou mayest dig brass.

DEUTERONOMY 8:9

And it shall come to pass,
that every living creature...
withersoever the rivers shall come,
shall live...

EZEKIEL 47:9

Rowing on the Yarkon River

...Stand in the gate of the LORD's house...
and say: Hear the word of the LORD...

JEREMIAH 7:2

The ancient synagogue at Capernaum on the shores of the Sea of Galilee

The Plain of Zebulun and the hills of Galilee seen from Mount Carmel

Zebulun shall dwell at the shore of the sea...

GENESIS 49:13

Har Tuv in the Judean hills: a cement factory

...Come, let us make brick...
And they had brick for stone...

GENESIS 11:3

*And the parched
land shall become
a pool...
It shall be an
enclosure for
reeds and rushes.*

ISAIAH 35:7

Lake Hulch

...I will climb up into the palm-tree,
I will take hold of the branches thereof...

THE SONG OF SONGS 7:9

And it came to pass, when the ark set forward,
that Moses said: 'Rise up, O LORD,
and let Thine enemies be scattered;
and let them that hate Thee flee before Thee.'

NUMBERS 10:35

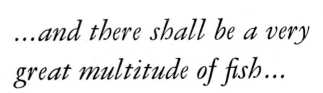

...and there shall be a very
great multitude of fish...

EZEKIEL 47:9

Gathering of members of the Israel Exploration Society at Subeita in the Negev

...Let us send men before us,
that they may search the land for us...

DEUTERONOMY 1:22

And Joshua turned back at that time, and took Hazor, and smote the king thereof with the sword...

JOSHUA 11:10

Hazor: a public building from the time of Ahab (9th century B.C.)

Haifa Port

*For Thou, L*ord, *hast made me glad through Thy work...*

PSALM 92:5

...The way of a ship in the midst of the sea...

PROVERB 30:19

Moreover there are workmen with thee in abundance,
hewers and workers of stone and timber,
and all men that are skilful in any manner of work...

I CHRONICLES 22:15

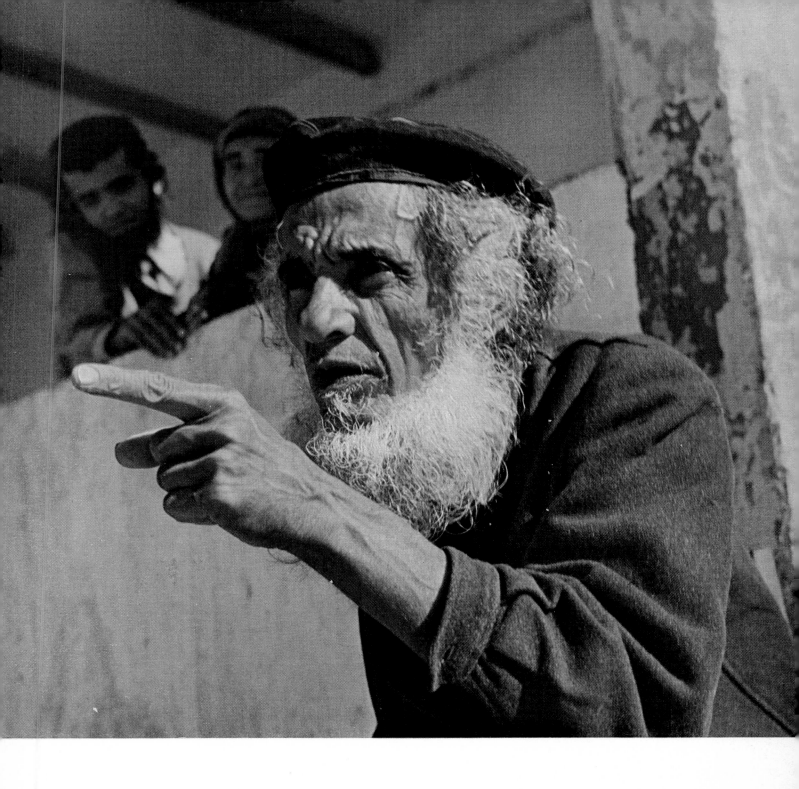

...And your sons and your daughters shall prophesy,
Your old men shall dream dreams...

JOEL 3:1

*...And his spring
shall become dry,
and his fountain
shall be dried up...*

HOSEA 13:15

*But ye, O mountains
of Israel, ye shall
shoot forth your branche
and yield your fruit to
My people, Israel...*

EZEKIEL 36:8

Parched land in the Negev

Lo, children are a heritage of the LORD...
As arrows in the hand of a mighty man...

PSALM 127:3-4

And the ransomed of the Lord shall return,
And come with singing unto Zion...

ISAIAH 51:11

For the LORD *thy God*
bringeth thee into a good land...
a land of olive-trees and honey...

DEUTERONOMY 8:7-8

Behold, the days come, saith the LORD*,*
That the plowman shall overtake the reaper...

A M O S 9 : 1 3

Frontier village: after the midday meal

...Come, eat of my bread,
And drink of the wine which I have mingled.

PROVERB 9:5

New housing outside Haifa

I made me great works; I builded me houses;
I planted me vineyards...
ECCLESIASTES 2:4

For God will save Zion, and build the cities of Judah;
And they shall abide there, and have it in possession.

PSALM 69:36

Jordan Valley settlements on the Sea of Galilee's southern shore

Beit Shearim, at the northern end of the Plain of Jezreel

In that day will I raise up
The tabernacle of David that is fallen...
And I will raise up his ruins...

AMOS 9:11

...And a fountain shall come forth
of the house of the LORD,
And shall water the valley of Shittim.

JOEL 4:18

National Water Carrier tunnel

And Lot lifted up his eyes, and beheld all the plain of the Jordan, that it was well watered every where...

GENESIS 13:10

And the border turned about...and went down to Bethshemesh, and passed along by Timnah.

JOSHUA 15:10

The "Pillars of Solomon" at Timna

Factory at Haifa Bay

*And it came to pass, that, when
the sun went down, and there was
thick darkness, behold a smoking furnace,
and a flaming torch...*

GENESIS 15:17

...I made me gardens and parks,
and I planted trees in them
of all kinds of fruit...

ECCLESIASTES 2:5

Young citrus plantations

...The flowers appear on the earth;
The time of singing is come,
And the voice of the turtle is heard in our land...

THE SONG OF SONGS 2:12

Thou gavest also Thy good spirit
to instruct them, and withheldest
not Thy manna from their mouth,
and gavest them water for their thirst.

NEHEMIAH 9:20

Immigrant children starting school

...I will make them hear My words...
that they may teach their children...

DEUTERONOMY 4:10

They that go down to the sea in ships,
That do business in great waters—
These saw the works of the Lord...

PSALM 107:23-24

...Write the vision,
And make it plain upon tables,
That a man may read it swiftly.

HABAKKUK 2:2

Then I went down to the potter's house, and,
behold, he was at his work on the wheels.

JEREMIAH 18:3

...and other of the Levites,
all that had skill with instruments of music.

II CHRONICLES 34:12

Paratroopers on parade

Drop down, ye heavens, from above,
And let the skies pour down righteousness...

ISAIAH 45:8

*So the workmen wrought, and the work
was perfected by them...*

II CHRONICLES 24:13

...As he that swimmeth spreadeth forth his hands to swim...

ISAIAH 25:11

Village school

...Teach a righteous man,
and he will increase in learning.

PROVERB 9:9

As cold waters to a faint soul,
So is good news from a far country.

PROVERB 25:25

Newsboy

*...Behold, I will bring it healing and cure,
and I will cure them...*   JEREMIAH 33:6

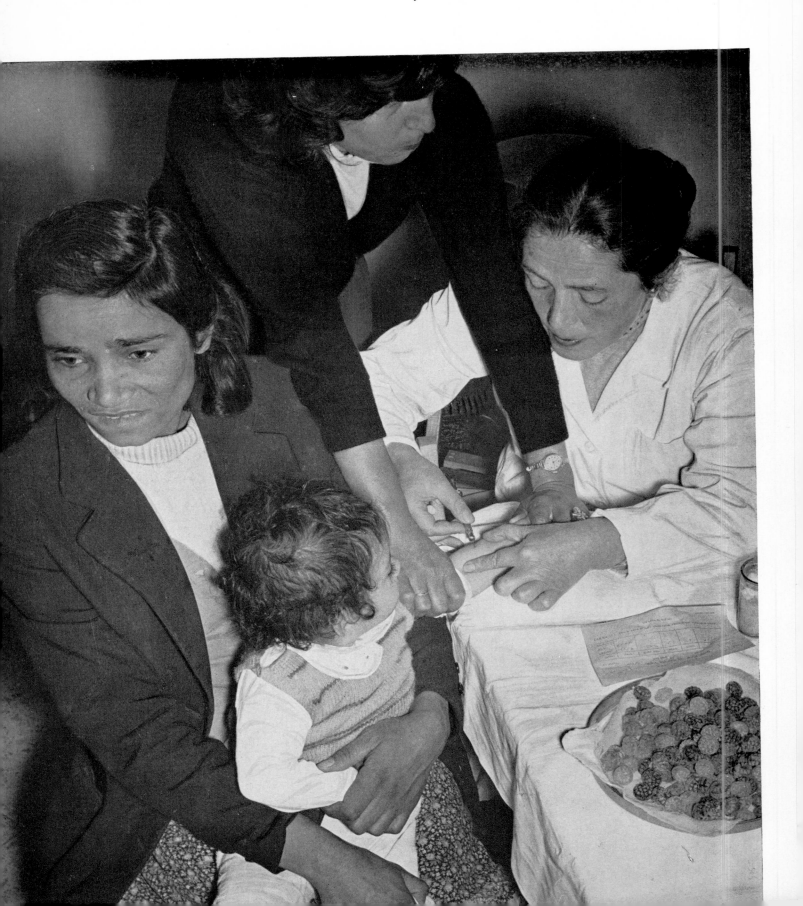

They run like mighty men...
And they entangle not their paths.

JOEL 2:7

Behold, thou art fair, my love...
Thy lips are like a thread of scarlet,
And thy mouth is comely...

THE SONG OF SONGS 4:1, 3

Thine is an arm with might;
Strong is Thy hand, and
    exalted is Thy right hand.

PSALM 89:14

Industry and its workers

The bellows blow fiercely,
The lead is consumed of the fire...

JEREMIAH 6:29

*...Rachel came with her father's sheep;
for she tended them.*

GENESIS 29:9

...A time to plant,
and a time to pluck up
that which is planted...

ECCLESIASTES 3:2

In the southern Negev

Highway through the hills

...Clear ye the way of the people;
Cast up, cast up the highway,
Gather out the stones...

ISAIAH 62:10

And a highway shall be there, and a way,
And it shall be called The way of holiness...
No lion shall be there,
Nor shall any ravenous beast go up thereon...

ISAIAH 35:8-9

Highway to Sodom

Ascent to Masada

Who shall ascend into the mountain of the Lord?
And who shall stand in His holy place?

PSALM 24:3

*And Isaac digged again
the wells of water, which
they had digged in the days
of Abraham his father...
And Isaac's servants digged
in the valley, and found there
a well of living water.*

GENESIS 26:18-19

...and their camels were without number,
as the sand which is upon the sea-shore for multitude.

JUDGES 7:12

Market day at Beersheba

Arise, shine, for thy light is come...

ISAIAH 60:1

...Naboth the Jezreelite had a vineyard,
which was in Jezreel,
hard by the palace of Ahab...

I KINGS 21:1

In the fields of Jezreel

...And for the tops of the ancient mountains,
And for the precious things of the everlasting hills,
And for the precious things of the earth and the fulness thereof...

DEUTERONOMY 33:15-16

Phosphate plant in Haifa

Sunflowers in the sand—Negev detail

En-Gedi: rocky fastness overlooking the Dead Sea

The wilderness and the parched land shall be glad;
And the desert shall rejoice, and blossom as the rose.

ISAIAH 35:1

...and they shall dwell safely in the wilderness...

EZEKIEL 34:25

Parade at Masada

...number thee an army...and we will fight against them in the plain, and surely we shall be stronger...

I KINGS 20:25

And men shall go into the caves of the rocks, And into the holes of the earth...

ISAIAH 2:19

Canyon near Eilat

And he said: 'Bring me a new cruse, and put salt therein.'

II KINGS 2:20

Skyline of Old Jaffa from the sea

Yonder sea, great and wide,
Therein are creeping things innumerable,
Living creatures, both small and great.

t works at Atlit

PSALM 104:25

...the acts of Hezekiah, and all his might, and how he made the pool, and the conduit, and brought water into the city...

II KINGS 20:20

Pipe factory

Highway and pipeline: life for the wilderness

...and they came and drew water, and filled the troughs to water their father's flock.

EXODUS 2:16

Water for man and beast in the Negev

And again I lifted up mine eyes, and saw...
two mountains; and the mountains were mountains of brass.

ZECHARIAH 6:1

Copper mines at Timna

New city in Galilee

Housing project near Jerusalem

*Moreover he built cities
in the hill-country of Judah,
and in the forest
he built castles and towers.*

II CHRONICLES 27:4

Conduit pipes for the National Water Carrier

And he stood by the conduit of the upper pool...

ISAIAH 36:2

Concrete wave barriers in Ashdod Port

Behold, I will do a new thing;
Now shall it spring forth; shall ye not know it?

ISAIAH 43:19

...and the cities shall be inhabited,
and the waste places shall be builded...

EZEKIEL 36:10

Haifa: the city and the port

...and there shall be with thee...
every willing man that hath skill,
for any manner of service...

I CHRONICLES 28:21

Thou also, son of man,
take thee a tile,
and lay it before thee...

EZEKIEL 4:1

Cobbler in Carmel Market

Tel Aviv stays awake on the eve of Independence Day   Leonard Bernstein conducts the famed Israel Philharmonic Orchestra

O clap your hands, all ye peoples;
Shout unto God with the voice of triumph.

PSALM 47:2

Sing unto the LORD *a new song...*
Let them sing praises unto Him with the timbrel and harp.

PSALM 149:1, 3

Be not afraid, ye beasts of the field;
For the pastures of the wilderness do spring...

JOEL 2:22

Mosaic pavement in the 6th-century
synagogue uncovered near kibbutz
Nirim in the Negev

New Israelis from Tunis
weaving carpets

...the weaver in colours,
in blue, and in purple, in scarlet,
and in fine linen...

EXODUS 35:35

When the righteous exult, there is great glory...

PROVERB 28:12

...with instruments of music,
psalteries and harps and cymbals, sounding aloud
and lifting up the voice with joy.

I CHRONICLES 15:16

Writers and artists at an Independence Day party   Israel Philharmonic Orchestra at the Tel Aviv Cultural Center

...as a bride adorneth herself with her jewels.

ISAIAH 61:10

Yemenite bride

side the Artists'
age at En-Hod

Then thou shalt see and be radiant...

ISAIAH 60:5

Torah scribe

Dead Sea Scrolls in the Shrine of the Book, Israel Museum

...and he was a ready scribe in the Law of Moses,
*which the L*ORD*, the God of Israel, had given...*

This book of the law shall not depart out of thy mouth,
but thou shalt meditate therein day and night...

JOSHUA 1:8

Druses' pilgrimage to the tomb of Nebi Shueib at Hattin (Sea of Galilee)

...the feast of harvest, the first-fruits
of thy labours,
which thou sowest in the field;
and the feast of ingathering...

EXODUS 23:16

...and, behold, a caravan
of Ishmaelites came from Gilead...

GENESIS 37:25

...For My house shall be called
A house of prayer for all peoples.

ISAIAH 56:7

Inside the Great Mosque at Acre   Inside the Church of the Dormition on Mount Zion

Synagogue at Hebrew University, Jerusalem

These things I remember,
*   and pour out my soul within me,*
How I passed on with the throng,
*   and led them to the house of God...*

PSALM 42:5

...Again shalt thou be adorned
*   with thy tabrets,*
And shalt go forth in the dances.
*   of them that make merry.*

JEREMIAH 31:4

A view of the Hula Plain

...*Who stretchest out the heavens like a curtain...*
Who makest the clouds Thy chariot,
Who walkest upon the wings of the wind...

...This land that was desolate is become like the garden of Eden...

EZEKIEL 36:35

A kibbutz in Jezreel

*...And there will be goats' milk
enough for thy food...*

PROVERB 27:27

The shepherd and his flock

...the children are tender,
and...the flocks and herds giving suck
are a care to me...

GENESIS 33:13

The earth is the Lord's, and the fulness thereof;
The world, and they that dwell therein.
For He hath founded it upon the seas,
And established it upon the floods.

PSALM 24:1-2

...I will hold Me still, and I will look on in My dwelling-place,
Like clear heat in sunshine...

ISAIAH 18:4

Jaffa: above the old port   Ruins of the ancient port of Caesarea

In the port

In the Negev

...For they shall suck the abundance of the seas,
And the hidden treasures of the sand.

DEUTERONOMY 33:19

And the channels of waters appeared,
And the foundations of the world were laid bare...

PSALM 18:16

Water channel in Galilee

He lieth under the lotus-trees,
In the covert of the reed, and fens.

JOB 40:21

Reeds in the Sea
of Galilee

*...My cities shall
again overflow
with prosperity...*

ZECHARIAH 1:17

*...and I after them...
upon the wall, above
the tower of the
furnaces, even unto
the broad wall...*

NEHEMIAH 12:38

And ye shall...proclaim liberty throughout the land unto all the inhabitants thereof; it shall be a jubilee unto you...

LEVITICUS 25:10

Independence regained

The Festival of the First Fruits at Gan Schmuel, in western Israel

Let the heavens be glad, and let the earth rejoice...
Let the field exult; and all that is therein;
Then shall all the trees of the wood sing for joy...

PSALM 96:11-12

...And let all the people
say: 'Amen.'
Hallelujah.

PSALM 106:48